STEWART WILLIAMS'

CARDIFF

YESTERDAY

1 *(Overleaf)* Members of the Health Committee of the Borough Council inspecting the first two steam propelled purpose-built 'motor wagons' for the Scavenging Section in the Old Town Hall Yard in St Mary Street on 12 April 1904. They were manufactured by the Mann Patent Wagon Company to the specification of the Scavenging Superintendent John Woosey and were capable of towing up to three ashcarts as well as the vehicle itself which could alternatively carry a detachable tank and watering apparatus

STEWART WILLIAMS'
CARDIFF
YESTERDAY

Book Twelve

**Introduction by
Geoff Dart**

First published September, 1985

© Stewart Williams, Publishers,
1 Trem-y-Don, Barry,
South Glamorgan

ISBN 0 900807 65 2

ACKNOWLEDGEMENTS

Our grateful thanks are extended to the following for kindly giving us permission to use their photographs:-

Mrs J. G. Ball 57; Mrs E. J. Bartlett 134, 135; Keith Batstone 35, 36, 41, 82, 98, 99, 151, 155, 157, 158, 211; Wm. H. Bishop 136, 195; Mrs Denise Capener 100, 101, 154; Cardiff Central Library 2, 8, 11, 12, 13, 14, 27, 28, 137, 138, 144, 145, 205; Ernie Carless 76, 77; Mrs Joan Case 53, 54, 55; Lionel Clode 50; Mrs Jo Coles 51, 52; R. F. Cooke 49; G. A. C. Dart 143; Mr & Mrs R. J. Daunton 32; Mrs Olwen Davies 78, 163; W. C. Davies 210; Mr & Mrs Reg Dobbins 94; Mrs K. Duddridge 152; Eddie Dumazel 64, 65, 66; Mrs Sylvia Edwards 169, 170, 171, 172, 212; Peter Evans 168; Bob Frank 90; Miss Reta Gale 9, 146, 180; Gladstone School Collection 140; Mrs Lilian Gooch 181; Mrs Marjorie Green 59, 83, 182, 183, 184, 185; Mr & Mrs John Griffiths 58, 86, 87, 88, 89, 141, 142; Ira Guy 29, 30; County Councillor Mrs A. Hill 81, 95, 153; C. W. Hill 131, 174; Sid Hill 15, 16, 17, 18; Mrs Grace Hosgood 156; Councillor Stan James 69, 91; Fred Jones 1, 3, 4, 5, 6, 21, 22, 23, 24, 25, 26, 42, 47, 48, 113, 130, 132, 133, 173, 175, 186, 188, 190, 191, 192, 193, 194, 196, 197, 203; Mr & Mrs E. J. King 61, 112, 166; William Langdon 109, 110, 111; Alan G. Lewis 10; W. O'Neill 67, 92, 93; Mrs Muriel Pearce 148; W. Penney 19, 20, 37, 38, 39, 40, 45, 46, 102, 103, 104, 105; Mrs Dorothy Powell 60; G. Powell 187; H. B. Priestley 122, 123; E. Rabaiotti 56; Mrs Valerie Redgrave 33, 34, 79, 120, 147, 149; J. E. Smith 96, 97, 178; Fred Stansfield 71, 72, 73, 74, 75; A. Syms 31; Mrs Joan Syms 179; Chris Taylor Collection 116, 117, 118, 119, 124, 125, 126, 127, 128, 129; Mrs Daisy Thompson 139; Mr & Mrs Eric Townsend 176, 177, 208, 209; Mrs M. Treble 189, 199; Mrs Betty Trezise 213, 214; Mrs K. Wade 121, 164; Alex Webb 43, 44, 68, 70, 84, 85, 106, 107, 108, 114, 115, 159, 160, 161, 162, 198, 200, 201, 204, 206, 207; G. Wheaton 80, 167; John Williams of Cardiff Ltd, 62, 63; Stewart Williams 7; J. F. Wilcox 150, 202; Howard Woon 165.

Endpapers: The Prince of Wales, accompanied by the Lord Lieutenant the Earl of Plymouth, in the semi-state coach, with military escort, passing under the Jubilee Arch in Kingsway en route to City Hall from the General Station on Saturday 11 May 1935. It was the highlight of a week of celebrations to mark the Silver Jubilee of King George V and Queen Mary
Courtesy Cardiff Central Library

Printed in Wales by D. Brown & Sons Ltd., Cowbridge and Bridgend, Glamorgan

Introduction

by Geoff Dart

The phenomenal growth of Victorian Cardiff, and the independent (until 1875) Roath and Canton, brought into existence an ever-expanding number of new streets for which names were selected by the landowner/developer, often using family and related names. After 1875 this resulted in many duplicated street-names in the enlarged Borough of Cardiff. In 1891 and on several subsequent occasions, the Head Postmaster complained about the confusion thus caused, whereupon the Borough Council took powers to control the naming of streets in the future and substituted, mostly in Roath and Canton, new names for those duplicated in the older town area. Such changes, however, were not confined to this decade or this reason. Memorable battles were fought over individual proposals; Crockherbtown in 1886-91 and Paradise Place in 1910 are examples. Conversely, some have been initiated by residents and have been approved without rancour; City Road in 1905 (originally Heol-y-Plwca or Plucca Lane, Castle Road from *c.* 1870), Avon Street (Halket Street until 1910) and others. In 1928 for the sake of monastic accuracy, the City Council changed Priory Street to The Friary and Priory to Friary Gardens.

As with all aspects of Cardiff's history, this name-changing brings to light interesting episodes which do not find a place in the history books. Here is a selection.

Howard Spring's birthplace. This world-famous novelist, who died in 1965, was known to have been born in 1889 in Edward Street and it was generally assumed to be the street of that name in the town centre, behind the late-lamented Capitol. In 1973 I received a letter from his old friend and journalistic colleague, the late David Prosser, in which he describes the novelist's last visit to Cardiff 1957/8. 'The last time he stayed with us he mentioned Edward Street as his birthplace as we were passing the Capitol Cinema. He said that it was thereabouts, but he had no recollection of the place for his early infancy was certainly in Canton.' In 1889, however, there were *two* streets of this name in Cardiff and his birth certificate shows that he was born at 32 Edward Street, *Canton*. There is a photograph of it in this book as Albert Street, its name after the 1891 'duplication' changes.

Sir William Goscombe John's birthplace. This renowned sculptor was also born in Canton, at the now-demolished 3 Union Street which was changed to Gray Street in 1891. Writing in 1894 from London to his friend the Chief Librarian, Mr. (later Sir) John Ballinger, he does not seem to be aware of this change. 'Now for the biography. Date of birth, 21st February 1860, in the classic spot of Union Street, Canton, Cardiff, don't know the number—that is awkward, for Union Street, Cardiff, may dispute the honour in the future.' His birth certificate confirms the place, but surprisingly, records the date as 21 March.

'The Pontcanna Party-Game'. The Head Postmaster included Glamorgan, Chester and Bangor Streets in his list of duplicate names, but the Borough Council did not have jurisdiction over the Pontcanna area east of Cathedral Road, which was then within the boundary of the Llandaff and Dinas Powis Rural District Council. In 1896 the latter agreed to change Bangor Street to Gileston Road, then being built, but refused to change

the other two on the grounds that they were in existence before the similarly-named streets in Canton and Grangetown. Stalemate ensued. Two Glamorgan Streets within less than a mile continued until 1923, soon after the City's boundaries were extended, when the Pontcanna one became Fairleigh Road. For some inexplicable reason it was March 1938 before the City Council resolved to change Chester Street, Pontcanna, to Maldwyn Street 'in view of the confusion with Chester Street, Grangetown.' Even this belated decision was not made without dissent—a resident suggested that the new name should be Cathedral Place.

'A Comedy of Errors'. The residents of Borstal Avenue, Heath, petitioned the Council in 1922 to change the name to the present Summerfield Avenue. Hardly surprising. It is odd, however, that in 1911, when the street was built, it should have received the name of a Kent village where the prototype young offenders' institution had been established in 1902. But could it have been an error? The other streets in the vicinity take the names of persons and places in the lineage of that ubiquitous family, Lewis of Van, from whom the landowner was descended. It does not mention Borstal in Kent, but it does include *Boarstall*, near Aylesbury, Bucks., a locality well-known to-day to naturalists and National Trust members for the preserved 18th century Boarstall Duck Decoy. A minor correction also seems to have been made in 1928/9 in the spelling of adjacent Clodien Avenue, formerly recorded as Clodian.

Finally, the good residents of Florence Street, Splott, would still be 'in Carey Street' if the Borough Council's original choice in 1896 had been permanent. It was changed just two months later at the request of William Bradley, a prominent solicitor.

AUTHOR'S NOTE

Cardiff has been fortunate to escape the worst excesses of the planners and developers who in the second half of the 20th century have managed to destroy much that was beautiful and historically valuable in many of our towns and cities. Few could argue against improving communications and providing better housing. But the thoughtless sweeping aside of some of our lovely old buildings must give cause for disquiet.

There is an element of nostalgia in all this, of course, and my postbag shows that to many who 'remember Cardiff as it was' even the most desirable redevelopments are sometimes resisted when they affect our own locality. Fortunately photographic evidence survives to remind us of 'Cardiff Yesterday' and this latest volume, like its eleven predecessors, contains many reminders of things as they used to be.

The sources of the illustrations are acknowledged elsewhere, but a special word of thanks must be due to all those people—and there are many hundreds—who have kept me supplied with so much splendid material over the past five years. In particular I owe a large debt of gratitude to Cardiff Central Library whose collection I have been privileged to draw from, and my good friend Fred Jones for his generosity in making so many superb postcards available to me. Bill Barrett, Chris Taylor, Dennis and Bill O'Neill have also worked tirelessly on my behalf and I am deeply grateful.

Finally my warm thanks to Geoff Dart, former County Librarian of South Glamorgan, to whom my indebtedness increases with each volume. In placing his considerable knowledge of the city's history at my disposal he has ensured that the series maintains an enviably high standard. And the last word must go to another old and valued friend, Geoff Rich, editor of the *South Wales Echo*, whose valuable advice and suggestions, invariably acted upon, have added much to the success of the series.

STEWART WILLIAMS   September, 1985

2 St Mary Street and High Street, *c.*1893. Sandwiched between Market Buildings and James Howell's is the *Borough Arms* (for many years known as the *Bodega*). It is said that the splendour of Market Buildings, built by Solomon Andrews to replace an earlier building destroyed by fire in 1885, so injured the pride of James Howell, whose premises had been until that time the tallest in St Mary Street, he rebuilt the *Borough Arms* to a greater height in an effort to pip his rival

Temperance Town, an area of small houses and narrow streets north of the General Railway Station, was so called because of a stipulation by the landowner, Colonel Edward Robert *Wood* of Stouthall, Gower, in his lease to Jacob *Scott* Matthews in 1858 that certain trades could not be carried out without his permission, including 'tavern keeper, alehouse keeper, or retailer of beer'. This suited Matthews who was a teetotaller—the first building he erected was the Temperance Hall (later Wood Street Congregational Chapel) and Raper's Temperance Hotel followed.

3 *(Right)* Marcovitch's grocery shop on the corner of Eisteddfod Street and Wood Street

4 *(Left)* On the left edge of this photograph of Wood Street is the goods entrance of C. Joseph & Company's warehouse. Their large premises 'Tudor House' contained departments dealing with jewellery and electro-plate; leather and fancy goods; glass, china and hardware; dolls, toys and games

5 Two more views of Temperance Town in the 1930s. *(Left)* Terminal Building now fills the site then occupied by the little shops on the right (south side) of Wood Street looking east towards St Mary Street

6 *(Right)* Wood Street Council School and St Dyfrig's Church are on the right. The school, opened in January 1879, became Cardiff Corporation Transport Department's offices after the Second World War. Together with St Dyfrig's it was demolished 1968-69 to allow the building of the new Wood Street bridge and the Transport and City Planning buildings

7   Prudential Assurance Building, Kingsway, soon after its opening in 1951. Behind it, partly hidden by trees, is the bombed rear of the Carlton Restaurant

8   St Mary Street in 1948. A Glamtax cab is in the foreground. Many will remember the maroon liveried Austins which operated from Westgate Street. The *Western Mail* and *South Wales Echo* moved to Thomson House in Havelock Street in 1960

9 This is Tudor *Street*, Riverside, *c*.1910. The tram poles were removed to the pavements *c*.1925.
Some of the properties on the left hand side of photograph were recently demolished to make way
for a block of Council flats

10 In the shadow of the castle wall in Kingsway a horse-drawn barge makes its way down the
Glamorganshire Canal to the Docks. A familiar sight in the 1920s when this was taken

11/12 Llystalybont farmhouse, *c.*1900. Situated at the lower end of Parkfield Place, Maindy, the building has been described as '19th century with an 18th century core'. It ceased to be a farm in 1918 when the land was taken for part of Mynachdy council estate. The farm building was then used for commercial purposes until the early 1970s when it fell into disrepair. Restored in 1983-84 in a MSC scheme for hostel accommodation for volunteers doing community work

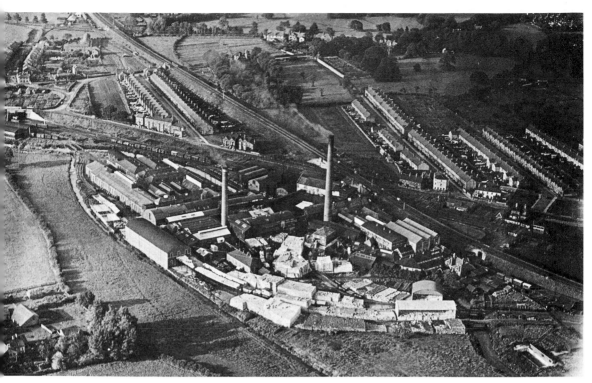

13/14 Aerial views taken in 1932. *(Above)* Thomas Owen's Ely Paper Works before Western Avenue was opened. The new Ely main line railway bridge can be seen top left; *(below)* the pontoon dock in the Roath Dock

15/16 Sid Hill was Cardiff Parks Department's Nursery Manager from 1947-1975, when he retired. Many will remember his glorious Autumn displays in the Chrysanthemum House *(above)* at Roath Park, a floral feature which was always marked by a presentation to the Lady Mayoress. In the early 1970s the Chrysanthemum House was replaced by the present Tropical House *(below)*

17/18 Opposite: *(Above)* Nursery Manager Hill with two of his assistants and some of the 2,500 pots of chrysanthemums on show; *(below)* The Lady Mayoress (Mrs Mary Robinson) being presented with a bouquet watched by among others the Lord Mayor (Alderman R. G. Robinson), Alderman R. G. Hill-Snook, W. Nelmes (Director of Parks), and Sid Hill, Autumn 1948

19 Wellington Street, Canton, between Albert Street and Picton Place, in the late 1960s. The prominent building is the YMCA Institute, originally a British School which closed *c.*1880 with the advent of state education and School Boards. It was taken over by the Salvation Army as their Canton Citadel *c.*1882 and later became Wellington Street Workmen's Institute

20 Albert Street with Cowbridge Road in the background. Howard Spring, the famous novelist, was born at No. 32. This whole area of Canton was demolished in the 1970s

Woodville Road, Cardiff. 1,019

21 Woodville Road, Cathays, *c.*1904

22 High Street, Llandaff, *c.*1909. On the left is the old village school; shops and offices now occupy the site screened by hoardings

Llandaff. High St. 83.

23 Clive Street, Grangetown, 1908. The sweet shop on the right is on the corner of Bromsgrove Street

24 The early years of the 20th century when sail was a common sight in the Docks

Bute West Basin Bute Docks. 253.

Entrance Hall
The John Cory Sailors' &
Soldiers' Rest., Cardiff

25/26   Built in 1901-02 the John Cory Sailors' and Soldiers' Rest at 179-180 Bute Street provided splendid recreational facilities for off-duty men in uniform. *(Above)* The flower-bedecked entrance hall with woodwork and brasses gleaming; *(below)* the English hall where first-class concerts were staged

English Hall   The John Cory Sailors' & Soldiers' Rest., Cardiff

27/28   The Taff Vale Railway Company's bridge across the Taff from the Docks to Grangetown
had been demolished when these views were taken *c.*1900. *(Above)* Site of the swing bridge over
the Glamorganshire Canal Sea Lock looking west with Sea Lock House on the right and Pomeroy,
Hunter and Burt Streets in the background; *(below)* sea wall where the road commenced on piles
near the Hamadryad Hospital ship, looking east towards the canal and beyond to Eleanor Street
Board School

29/30 For many years the Guy fleet of tugs looked after the navigational needs of shipping using the port of Cardiff. The family lived in Windsor Esplanade and 'Tommy the Fish' Letton numbered them among his customers. He remembers David Guy as 'the man who always wore a flower in his buttonhole'. *(Right)* An early trade card issued by the Company; *(below) The Rose* seen in the West Dock with Neale & West's fish quay and the Norwegian Church on the left and the funnel of a N. & W. trawler on the right

31 When this was taken in the 1930s Cardiff described itself as 'the leading coal exporting port of the world'. Even so trade had declined from 24½ million tons in 1913—the peak year of South Wales coal shipments—to less than 11 millions in 1938. This was partly due to the substitution of oil for coal in ships and railway locomotives and partly to the subsidising by foreign governments of their coal exports. The extent of Cardiff's dependence on coal can be gauged from an analysis of the figures of exports and imports in 1936 which show that 97½% of exports consisted of coal, coke and patent fuel. Now, half a century later, there are few reminders of those great days

32 Loaves in the oven, others waiting their turn, and a slab of currant cake for good measure . . . a peep into Edmund Minifie's bakery at 27 Severn Road at the turn of the century (note the assistant's freshly starched apron). Edmund also ran a grocery business from the same address

33/34   J. R. Freeman & Son opened a cigar factory in Bridge Street in 1908. Later they moved to Grangetown and it was here in 1912 that the famous Manikin cigars were first produced, possibly by some of the girls seen *(above)* during the First World War and *(below)* in the early 1920s. The present factory in Penarth Road was opened in 1961

35/36 Pre-war staff employed by Marks & Spencer. *(Above)* Outside the Queen Street store before departing on an outing in 1936; *(below)* enjoying a breather on the roof during the summer of 1937

37/38 The area bounded by Wellington Street, Cowbridge Road and Leckwith Road was considered 'ripe for development' from the mid 1960s. It was an area liberally provided with pubs. In addition to the four shown on these pages, there were also originally in Wellington Street the *Wellington* and *Swan*

39/40 *(Above)* Standing on the step outside *The Greyhound*, on the corner of Wellington Street and North Morgan Street, is 'mine host' Jimmy Nelson, Cardiff City's brilliant Scottish international right back; *(below)* the *Duke of York* in Wellington Street which closed on 30 April 1975

41 Bill Batstone, greengrocer and fishmonger, with his horse and cart in Universal Street, Grangetown, *c.*1927

42 When ginger beer was sold in stone jars . . . Lowe Brothers, Pontcanna, delivery cart with the firm's manager, *c.*1910. Lowe's occupied the first house in Glamorgan Street (now Fairleigh Road)

43/44   W. Oakes, grocer and provision merchant, was in business at 37 Wells Street, Canton, for half a century until the early 1950s. Deliveries were made over a wide area and one of his drivers, Ernie Pluck, is seen in both photographs. *(Above)* With horse and cart on Llantrisant Road in 1919, and *(below)* in the early 1920s with a newly-delivered van. The lad on the right is Bill Call who later ran his own greengrocery business in Wells Street

45 Donald Knight founded a drapery business in 1889 which became well known throughout the city. This section of Cowbridge Road East was originally called Romilly Terrace, a group of upper-class residences built in the mid-1850s. Knight's business folded in 1970 and is now the site of International Stores supermarket

46 Ind Coope's office and stores on the corner of Cowbridge Road and Radnor Road 'for sale' after the Burton company moved to Marshfield in 1963. The frontage was later developed with shop-fronts and a public house, *The Maltings*, which took its name from the massive malthouse on the Radnor Road frontage built by a local brewer in the early 1870s. In 1890 it was known as Dowson's Malthouse

47 Charlie Richards' grocery shop on the corner of Montgomery Street and Angus Street, Roath, *c*.1910

48 Charles Banwell ran the Cardiff Dairy Company from 47 Atlas Road, Canton, in 1927

49 Western Mail Tudor Printing Works staff outing to Llantwit Major in 1922

50 Shipping butchers from all over South Wales (many from Cardiff) had a field day at Symonds Yat in 1930

51 Fred Saddler's shaving saloon in Holmesdale Street, Grangetown, 1900

52 Sparkes' Garage, Penhill Road, in the 1940s. Now the site of Penhill House

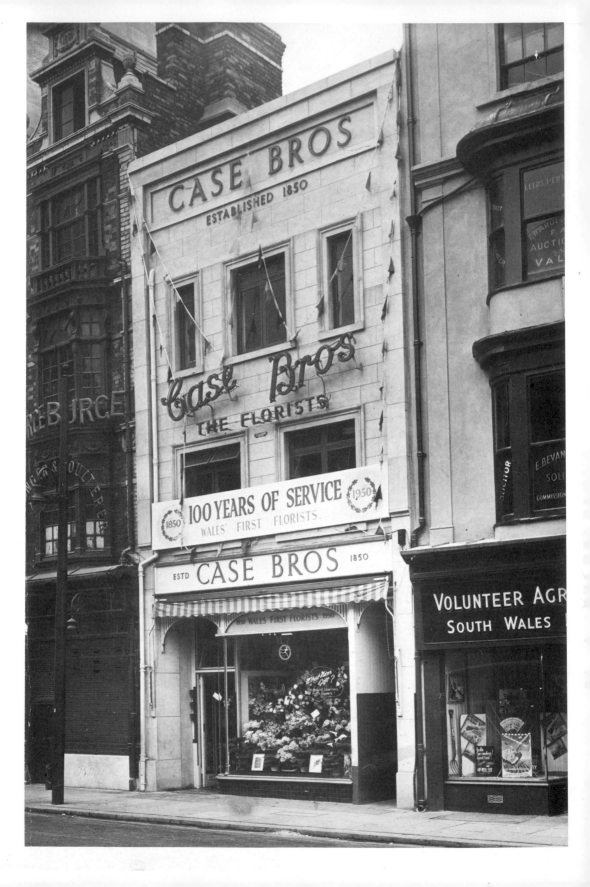

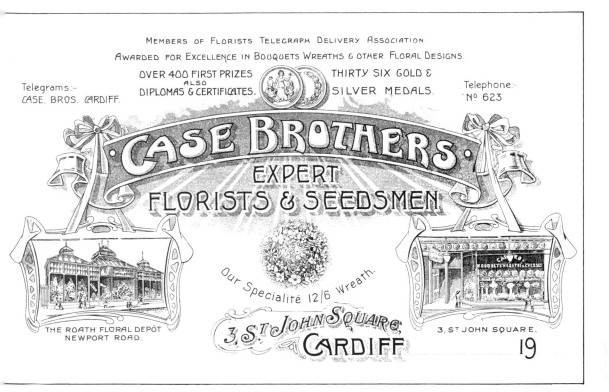

53/54/55 Founded in 1850 and still going strong, Case Brothers—Wales' First Florists—has been passed down from father to son in an unbroken line since Fred Case came over with a brother from Somerset and set up as a greengrocer and florist. At different times the firm has traded from 35-37 Queen Street, 21 High Street, 3 St John Square, 40 Castle Arcade and 103 Cathays Terrace. In addition they have had nurseries at Rumney (on the County Cinema site), 113 Newport Road (shown on the above bill-head) and Lisvane.

(Left): The St John Square shop decorated for the firm's centenary in 1950

(Right): The Lord Mayor (Alderman Robert Bevan) with the floral tribute for King George VI from the City of Cardiff

56 Opened in 1927, 'Bert' Rabaiotti's cafe at the southern end of St Mary Street was a popular rendezvous noted for its delicious coffee and ice cream which many Cardiffians will remember with affection. It closed in 1941

57 The Union Jacks in the window of Blackweir Post Office, North Road, and the little boy making sure his flag is in the picture give a clue to the occasion—the Silver Jubilee of King George V and Queen Mary in 1935

58   Office staff employed by Thomas Owen & Co. Ltd, at Ely Paper Mills, 1957

59   Employees of Preston & Thomas Ltd, fish range makers, outside the firm's Minny Street premises in the 1930s. They moved there from Caroline Street c.1927-28. Now located at Greenway Road, Rumney, where they moved in 1974-75

60 G. R. Phillips' pork butcher's shop on the corner of Woodville Road and Crwys Road, 1929. The site is now occupied by Crwys House

61 Staff employed in Curran's electrical department pose outside the firm's machine tools factory in 1940

62/63 The social side of John Williams & Sons (Cardiff) Ltd. *(Above)* Staff about to depart for the Annual Welfare Outing to London on 24 September 1955; *(below)* Sidney Roberts and pals enjoying a drop of the local brew in the Civic Centre at a Welfare function in 1928

Sport and Entertainment

64 Canton-born Eddie Dumazel was seven years old when he joined Cardiff City Boxing Club in 1930. Valuable experience gained there and later with Cardiff Gas helped to shape him into a stylish and capable featherweight. Eddie joined the RAF in 1941 and continued to box whenever possible impressing among others Len Harvey, the British heavyweight champion who was serving as an officer. Following demobilisation in 1946 he turned professional and in 1947 went to America where he had 16 fights, winning twelve of them. In the course of his professional career Eddie Dumazel had some 70 fights and won the majority. Although top honours eluded him he will be remembered as a courageous contender who added sparkle to many boxing promotions

65   Eddie Dumazel at the height of his career

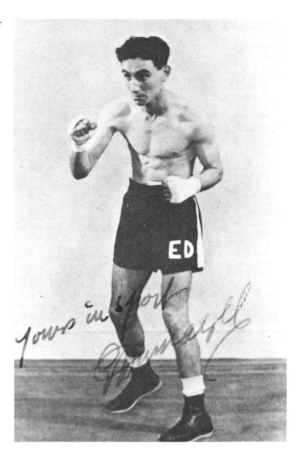

66   A ringside view of Eddie Dumazel as he puts down Ben Duffy in their featherweight contest at Blackpool Circus in 1948

67 The sporting Burns family, related to World featherweight champion 'Peerless Jim' Driscoll, turned out in strength for Billy Burns wedding in 1932. In this group are brothers Jim 'Ocker' Burns, who played rugby for Cardiff and Wales, and Tom, a schoolboy international who also played for Cardiff RFC. Their father kept the *Duke of Edinburgh* hotel in Newtown, where 'Peerless Jim' died, and at one time managed the legendary fighter

68 The Prior family of Canton—father, four sons and son-in-law—with some of their trophies gained from air rifle shooting

69 *Westgate Inn* (on the corner of Angelina Street and Frances Street, Docks) Skittles Club, 1929-30. Champions of the Cardiff City Table Skittles League and winners of the Ind Coope Cup

70 *Boar's Head* bagatelle team, cup and shield winners, 1936-37. Third from left, back row, is 'Professor' Sweeney, owner of the Pavlova Ballroom, Leckwith Road, and a Welsh dancing champion

(Opposite) The moment 30,000 fans have been waiting for as Fred Stansfield leads his team on to Ninian Park for another thrilling game during Cardiff City's magnificent 1946-47 season

72 Proud moment for Fred Stansfield, Cardiff City's captain, as he holds the Football League Division III Championship Shield after the Bluebirds' highly successful 1946-47 season. They won 30, drew 6 and lost 6 of their 42 games, scoring 93 goals

The 1946-47 Championship team. *(Back row, left to right)* Ken Hollyman, Bob Allison (trainer), Stan Richards, Dan Canning, Glyn Williams, Billy Rees, Bryn Allen, Roy Clarke; *(middle)* Colin Gibson, Arthur Lever, Fred Stansfield, Alf Sherwood, George Wardle; *(front)* Billy Baker, Bernard Ross

74 Moscow Dynamo FC made a short tour of Britain in November 1945. They played Cardiff City at Ninian Park before a crowd of 45,000, and beat them 10-1. The Russian skipper Semichastny is seen presenting City captain Fred Stansfield with a bouquet of flowers before the game. The Bluebirds reciprocated by presenting each Dynamo with a miniature miner's lamp

75 Fred Stansfield *(left)* joined Cardiff City in 1942. He made 106 league appearances and captained the side in 1946-47 when they won the Third Division Championship. Remembered as a fine centre-half who was always difficult to beat, he was also a great sportsman and a splendid ambassador for the City. Capped for Wales against Scotland in 1949

76/77 Older Cardiff City supporters will remember the clever ball play and never-say-die spirit of Ernie Carless who joined the Bluebirds in the 1930-31 season. *(Above)* Ernie, far left, chases a half-chance against Exeter City at Ninian Park in 1931; *(below)* equally at home on the cricket field, Ernie played some games for Glamorgan and turned out for Devon while with Plymouth Argyle in the late 1940s. He is seen here captaining a Cardiff side in a friendly game at Bridgend in August 1949

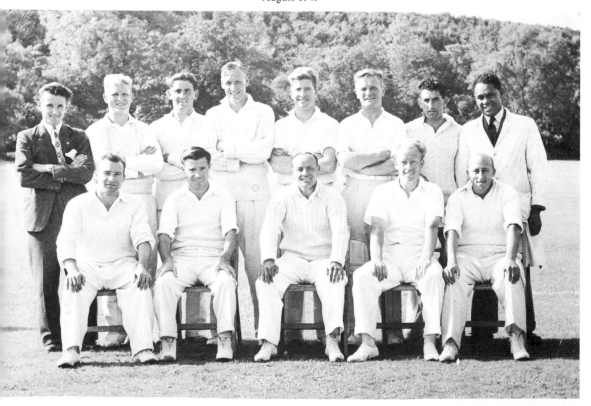

78   Conway Road Methodist Church soccer team, *c.*1912

79   Adamsdown School soccer team, 1925-26

ADAMSDOWN
1925-26

80   Radnor Road School soccer XI, 1950-51 season

81   Cardiff Schools' Football League Junior XI 1955 56, Diamond Jubilee Year. Captain is
R. Alderman

82   Splott Old Boys' soccer team, 1930-31, at Splott Park

83   Preston & Thomas Ltd, soccer team 1937

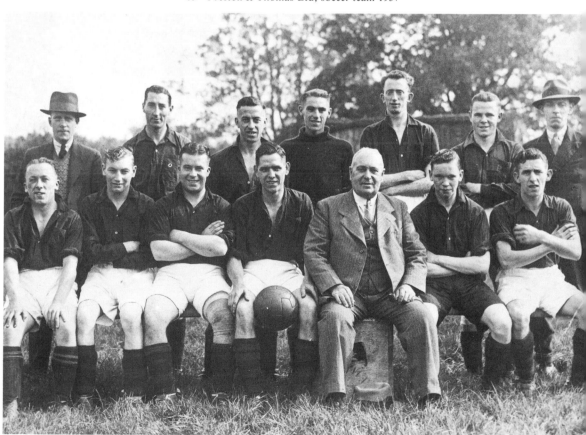

84 Leckwith Ninians FC, 1938. Captain is Ken Savage

85 Canton Corries FC at Jubilee Park during the 1946-47 season. Captain is Ron Jones

86　Cardiff Cycle Speedway Championship match at Menelaus Street, Splott Moors, in 1954

87　Cardiff Hammers Cycle Speedway team with their trophies, 1955

88/89 Jimmy Wright *(left)* and Gerald Pugh, popular members of Cardiff Dragons speedway team, seen at Cardiff Stadium, Penarth Road, in 1951

90 Waiting for a signal from the starter. Youngsters in Archer Crescent, Ely, enjoying a 'make believe' speedway race with machines made from old bicycle frames and pram wheels in 1930. The donor, Bob Frank, is on the extreme left

CITY OF CARDIFF

CORPORATION BATHS

CARDIFF

Lord Mayor's Certificate

Initiated by

Alderman Illtyd Thomas, J.P., Lord Mayor, 1907-8.

This is to Certify that

H. E. Hunter

has acquired the art of SWIMMING, having

qualified for a distance of 440 yards at these Baths.

Date 22ⁿᵈ July 1918. J. L. Wheatley Town Clerk.

Countersigned J. W. Duncan. Manager of Baths,
Guildford Crescent,
Cardiff.

Nº _____

(Opposite) Many hundreds of these proficiency certificates—an idea initiated by Alderman Illtyd Thomas during his term as Lord Mayor in 1907-08—were awarded to young swimmers at Guildford Crescent Baths when they 'acquired the art of swimming'. This one belonged to H. E. Kimber and must be one of very few to have survived

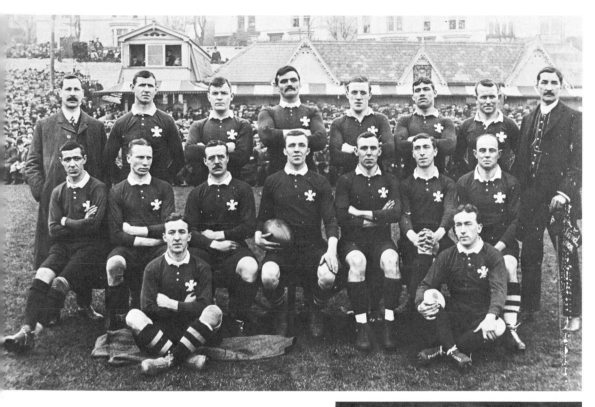

92/93 *(Above)* The famous Wales rugby XV 1907-08, Triple Crown, Championship, and first-ever Grand Slam winners, contained eight Cardiff RFC players—W. O'Neill, J. A. Brown, P. F. Bush, J. L. Williams, H. B. Winfield, R. T. Gabe, R. Gibbs and A. F. Harding. *(Right)* The Triple Crown medal which was presented to each member of the team

94   Williams House rugby team, Canton High School, 1943-44

95   Howardian Hornets XV 1957-58, winners of the Western Mail Shield

96   Cathays High School 1st XV, 1949-50. Record—played 21, won 15, drew 3, lost 3: points for
268, against 69

97   Cathays High School Old Boys' rugby XV who defeated a Barcelona team 3-0 at Cardiff
Arms Park in 1963

98   Allensbank Junior School rugby team, 1954-55 season

99   Allensbank Junior School baseball team, 1955

100/101 Eleanor Street School sports groups. *(Above)* Girls' baseball team, 1951; *(below)* netball team, 1953

102 County Cinema, Rumney, was opened on Boxing Day 1939. Declining business due to changing public taste in entertainment resulted in its closure in November 1974. Since then the building has steadily deteriorated while arguments continue over its future

103 Splott Cinema was opened in 1913. Films were last shown there on 2 September 1961. From that date it has operated as a Bingo Club

104/105 The western suburb of Ely boasted two cinemas. *(Above)* The Regent in Mill Road opened in 1929 and screened its last films on 2 September 1961. Now a Bingo Club; *(below)* the Avenue in Cowbridge Road West opened on 12 February 1940 and closed in 1961. Presently owned and used by Howells as a Rolls Royce and Porsche car showroom

106 Young members of the Trelai School of Dancing, Ely, go through their paces at Trelai Community Hall, c. 1957

107/108 Hundreds of talented young Cardiff dancers had their first taste of 'show biz' with Madam Beaton's dancing troupes who were featured in many New Theatre pantomimes and appeared in shows throughout Wales. Both of these groups were appearing at the New Theatre *(above)* as the Juveniles in 1943, and *(below)* as Madam Beaton's Young Ladies in 1948

109 The Novello Singers with their musical director Miss Eira Novello Williams *(left)* and accompanist Miss Marion Williams on stage at the Empire Theatre where they were appearing for a week in the early 1950s as part of a promotion for Charlie Chaplin's film 'Limelight'. Formed in 1945, the Singers have appeared many times on radio and television and are still kept busy with concerts and charity performances

110/111   The Snowflakes juvenile choir occupies a special place in Cardiff's musical history. Formed in 1926, for over half a century they gave enormous pleasure to thousands of Cardiffians. *(Above)* At Llangollen International Eisteddfod in the early 1950s where they were among the prize-winners; *(below)* the full choir with musical director Miss Eira Novello Williams *(left)* and accompanist Miss Marion Williams. Soprano Ira Stevens *(fourth left, front row)* was at one time in the 1930s an understudy to child film star Shirley Temple in Hollywood

112 The Cardiff Banjo, Mandoline and Guitar Band, popular entertainers in the 1930s when novelty musical combinations were fashionable

113 Ballads on a sunny summer's afternoon at Roath Park Pavilion. Many concert parties performed here between the wars, perhaps the best remembered being Waldini and his Gypsy Band

114/115 Concert Parties were enormously popular in the 1920s and 30s when live entertainment attracted eager audiences. Western hits like 'Home on the Range' and 'Old Faithful' were the rage and this Canton Party boasted its own 'Singing Cowboy', Ernie Gray, who is seen *(right)* in stetson and chaps, and *(below)* in more formal dress with guitar. Off stage Ernie worked for the GWR at Canton loco sheds

Transport

116 A Daimler CVD6 double-decker with East Lancs bodywork undergoing a tilt test after the body had been transferred from a Leyland chassis by Cardiff Corporation in 1948

117 Cardiff Corporation Leyland 'Titan' 48-seater 'o trial' in St John Square. It was eventually purchased 1931 and sold to Southern Vectis, Isle of Wight, in 194

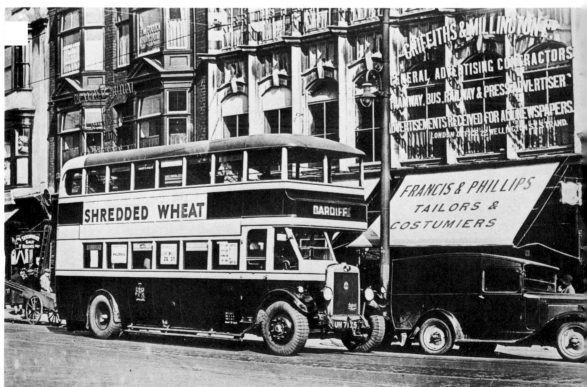

118/119 Obverse and reverse sides of a handbill issued by the Transport Department in August 1945. PAYE was first introduced on the trolleybus system in 1942. In the following year it was extended to the trams and in 1945 it was employed on Victoria Park and Ely bus services. By 1950 heavy losses due to the low flat fare—not helped by the dishonest few who had a field day—led to the abandonment of the scheme

Cardiff Corporation Transport Dept.

VICTORIA PARK & ELY BUS SERVICES

Pay As You Enter!

No Change Given!

4/45. W.M. 406.

The Public are notified that, commencing **SUNDAY, 19th AUGUST,** 1945, the **PAY AS YOU ENTER** system of fare collection will be operated on the following services :—

Nos. 26b, 27b, 35b, Victoria Park and Snowden Road. Marcross Road and Culverhouse Cross.

The P.A.Y.E. system will operate on the "short running" services between **Victoria Park** and **Ely** only, and the "ticket issue" method will be maintained on all buses operating the through services between G.W.R. (Gen. Station) and Ely.

In consequence of the operation of P.A.Y.E. on the Victoria Park to Ely Section certain fares will be reduced and, for the information of the Public, revised Fare List is set out on the back hereof.

VICTORIA PARK and SNOWDEN RD., MARCROSS RD. or CULVERHOUSE CROSS

ONE FARE ONLY 1D.

SERVICES Nos. 26a, 27a, 35a.

G.W.R. (Gen. Station) and SNOWDEN ROAD ; MARCROSS ROAD ; CULVERHOUSE CROSS.

REVISED FARE LIST.

Stage No.	St. Georges-super-Ely	Ty Llwyd Farm	Culverhouse Cross or Snowden Road	Marcross Road	Amroth Rd., Caerau Sq. or Charteris Rd.	Grand Ave. (Cowbridge Rd.) or Heol-y-Felin (Mill Rd.)	Aldsworth Road	Victoria Park	Grosvenor Street	Beda Road	Ninian Park Hotel	Smeaton Street	Tudor Street Junction	G.W.R. (Gen. Stn.)
1	St. Georges-super-Ely													
2	1	Ty Llwyd Farm												
3	1	½	Culverhouse Cross or Snowden Road											
4	2	1	1	Marcross Road										
5	2	2	1	1	Amroth Rd., Caerau Sq. or Charteris Rd.									
6	3	2	2	1	1	Grand Ave. (Cowbridge Rd.) or Heol-y-Felin (Mill Rd.)								
7	3	3	2	2	1	1	Aldsworth Road							
8	3	3	2	2	1	1	1	Victoria Park						
9	4	3	2	2	1½	1	1	1	Grosvenor Street					
10	4	3	3	2	1½	1½	1	1	1	Beda Road				
11	4	4	3	2	2	1½	1½	1	1	1	Ninian Park Hotel			
12	4	4	3	2½	2	2	1½	1½	1	1	1	Smeaton Street		
13	4½	4	3½	2½	2	2	2	1½	1½	1	1	1	Tudor Street Junction	
14	5	4	4	3	2½	2	2	2	1½	1½	1	1	1	G.W.R. (Gen. Stn.)

Ordinary Return Fare :
G.W.R. (Gen. Station) and Grand Ave. (Cowbridge Rd.) or Heol-y-Felin (Mill Rd.) : **5d. R.**

Concessional Rates, viz.: Workpeople's Returns, Child's Special and School Returns and Season Tickets will not be issued for travel between Victoria Park and Ely Terminal points, but will be maintained as at present, for travel between Victoria Park and Town Centre.

On P.A.Y.E. BUSES (viz., buses operating "short running" journeys between Victoria Park and the Ely termini), TICKETS WILL NOT BE ISSUED ; CHANGE WILL NOT BE GIVEN, and Passengers must have the EXACT FARE of ONE PENNY ready BEFORE boarding.

120 Tram conductresses employed by the City Transport Department outside the National Museum of Wales in 1946

121 Opening of the City Transport Bus Garage in Sloper Road by the Lord Mayor (Alderman R. G. Hill-Snook) on 29 July 1931. S. H. Lewis, structural engineer with Dawnays who supplied the steelwork, is handing the Lord Mayor a scissors to cut the tape, watched by William Forbes (Transport Manager), George H. Whitaker (City Engineer) and A. Hollyman (Dawnays)

122/123 *(Above)* A 2a Victoria Park—Newport Road tram negotiating the single-line track east of King's Road in Cowbridge Road, Canton, April 1939; *(below)* another tram on the same route passing Matthews' and The Trico ice cream parlors at Victoria Park

124/125 Trolleybuses—'Cardiff's silent service'—were an important part of the city's transport system from March 1942, when they were first introduced, until January 1970, when they were finally abandoned. *(Above)* Trolley passing under Rhymney railway bridge (demolished on 12 October 1967) on its way from St Mary Street to Gabalfa; *(below)* another from the mid-1960s turning into Adelaide Street from James Street, Docks, on the Gabalfa–Pier Head service

126/127 *(Above)* City Road junction in early 1966. Note the Hodge Building under construction; *(below)* testing new trolleybus wiring in Dumfries Place, part of an extensive rewiring operation for the Queen Street one-way system, in mid-1965

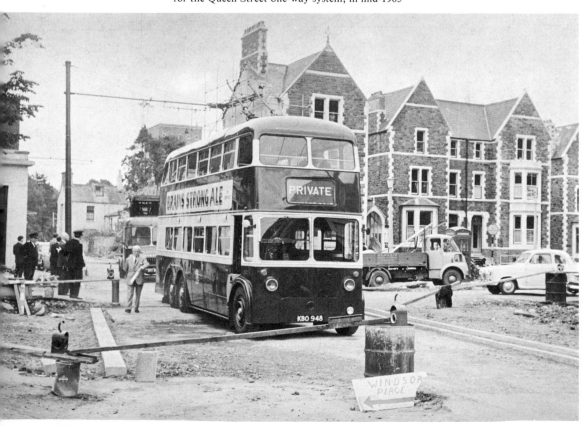

128/129 Before the abandonment of the trolleybus system in 1970 Cardiff Corporation Transport Department gave the National Trolleybus Association permission to operate 'foreign' rolling stock over some routes.
(Left) Bournemouth Corporation BUT six-wheel trolleybus outside the *Angel Hotel*; *(below)* Glasgow Corporation single-decker, one of the first over 30ft long four-wheel vehicles in Great Britain, turning into High Street

130   Grangetown signal box in the 1940s

131   Engineman and shunters at Newtown West End railway sidings in the late 1920s

PARK MOTOR GARAGE

132/133   Between 1910 and 1914 D. Brian ran a fleet of cars for hire from his Park Motor Garage in Richards Terrace, Roath. The business card *(above)* gives an indication of the comprehensive service available to those who could afford the luxury of hiring or owning a motor car before the First World War

134/135 For 50 years, from 1919 until his retirement in 1969, Eddie Bartlett operated a taxi business, principally from the *Royal George* garage, Mackintosh Place, Roath. He was for many years honorary secretary of the South Wales and Monmouthshire Public and Private Car Hire Association. *(Above)* Eddie with his first taxi, a 1912 Belsize; *(below)* a pair of Austin saloons outside the City Hall for a society wedding in the 1930s

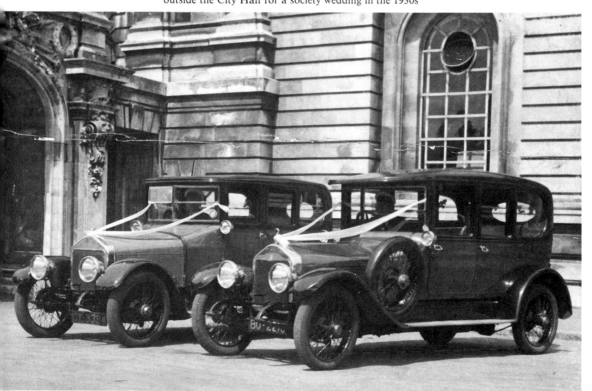

136 James Clark, haulage contractor, displays his fleet prior to providing transport for a Whitsun Treat. With him is his grand-daughter Doreen. Clynes Street, Gorton, c.1925.

Religion, Education and Public Service

137 Hannah Street Congregational Chapel in Butetown was built in 1867 to the designs of Architects W. G. Habershon and A. R. Pite. With its neo-Greek façade and Corinthian columns it has been described as 'one of the best-looking chapels in Cardiff'. Sadly it had a short life of 50 years. Because of dwindling congregations it was sold in 1917 and became a warehouse. Demolished in the 1960s

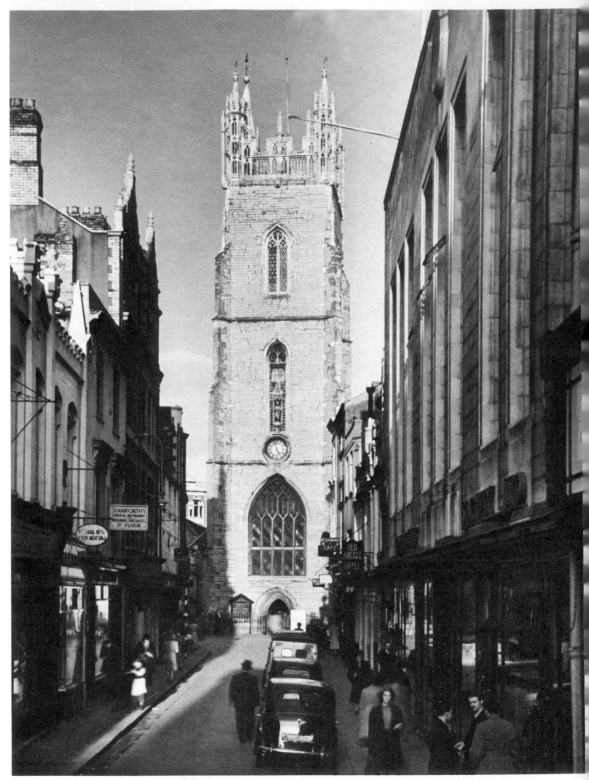

138 The graceful perpendicular west tower of St John the Baptist's Church, designed by John Hart in 1473, seen from Church Street in 1948. The building on the extreme left over the shops was a Wesleyan Methodist Chapel rebuilt in 1829 to replace a smaller late 18th century chapel which in turn is almost certain to have replaced on the same site the first Wesleyan methodist 'room' or chapel founded in Wales

139 Ely Methodist Church Sisterhood outside the new church building opened in May 1911

140 St Michael's Church Fete held at Gelligaer Street, August 1924

141/142   Corpus Christi procession in Cardiff, 1960. *(Above)* Pupils of St Francis RC School, Ely; *(below)* Form V, St Illtyd's College

143 Sherwood House, Newport Road. It was built in 1876 for Archibald Hood, one of South Wales' leading coalowners. In 1933, when this was taken, it had become St Illtyd's College House, the residence of the Brothers De La Salle teaching order. Demolished in 1966, it is now the site of Telephone House

144/145 The opening of the Tatem physics and chemistry laboratories at University College, Cathays Park, on 21 May 1930. *(Opposite)* HRH the Prince of Wales, who performed the opening, with the Lord Mayor (Alderman W. Charles)

146   Prefects, Cathays High School for Girls, 1939

147   Form 4c, Lady Margaret High School, 1953. This school, built in Colchester Avenue in 1939, was occupied by the military throughout the war. Released in 1948, it resumed as Lady Margaret until the reorganisation of 1972-73 when it was merged with Howardian High School

148   Pupils of Adamsdown Infants' School, 1924

149   Girls and boys from Adamsdown School at Splott Park in 1931

150   Members of Adamsdown School Old Boys' Association making a nostalgic return visit to
'the old school' on 18 March, 1959

151   Standard 4a, Allensbank Junior School, 1954-55

152 Pupils of the Canton National School, Leckwith Road, 1926

153 Pupils of Despenser Gardens Preparatory School, 1952

154　Pupils of Eleanor Street School, 1946

155　Top class, Grange Council Infants' School, 1919

156 Pupils of Grange Council School, 1935-36

157 Top class, Gladstone Infants' School, 1922

158 Standard 1, Gladstone Junior School, 1922

159 Standard 1b, Kitchener Road Infants' School, 1929

160 Standard 3, Kitchener Road School, 1932

161 Pupils of Kitchener Road Infants' School, 1926

162 Standard 1, Kitchener Road School, 1939-40

163 Pupils of Lansdowne Road Infants' School, 1942

164   Pupils of Marlborough Road Elementary School, 1923-24

165   Standard 1, Moorland Road Junior School, 1927. The donor's father, 'Big Windsor Woon' *(fourth left, back row)*, then seven, is a well-known Cardiff personality

166   Pupils in fancy dress at Roath Park Infants' School in 1935

167   Pupils of Radnor Road School, 1939

168 Pupils from Radnor Road, Adamsdown, and Metal Street Schools at Porthcawl Camp, May 1949

169 Pupils of Rhiwbina School, 1942

170   Pupils of Rhiwbina School, 1943

171   Pupils of Rhiwbina School, 1946

172   Class 3, Rhiwbina School, 1945

173   Standards 4 and 5, Rumney Council School, 1919, with headmaster James Mathewson

174   Pupils of Stacey Road School, 1930-31

175   Pupils of St Mary the Virgin (National) School, 1927-28

176   Pupils of Severn Road Infants' School, 1937

177   Pupils of Severn Road Junior School, 1938-39

178   Standard 4a, Windsor-Clive Junior School, 1962

179   Pupils of Windsor-Clive School, Ely, at Porthcawl Camp, November 1949

PORTHCAWL CAMP. NOV. 1949.

180 Two generations of the Gale family—John and his son Tony—serving together in Cardiff City Police, c.1920

181 Doris Gooch rescued a four-year-old girl, Sandra Tottal, from drowning in the Glamorganshire Canal in March 1949. The brave deed led to this presentation of the Parchment of the Royal Humane Society by Councillor E. J. Cazenave at Eleanor Street School. Others in the group with Doris are her mother, schoolteachers and Assistant Chief Constable W. F. Thomas

182/183 Second World War VIP inspections of Cardiff firemen. *(Above)* The Duke of Kent, accompanied by Chief Constable James Wilson, on a visit to Insole Court in October 1940; *(below)* NFS on parade for Home Secretary, the Rt. Hon. Herbert Morrison, also at Insole Court, in 1942

184/185 Five Cardiff firemen were killed in one of the most vicious fires of the Second World War. It happened on 19 August 1940 when three German Junkers 88s made a low level attack against the Admiralty oil tanks at Pembroke Dock. The fire raged for three weeks and was fought by 650 men from 22 brigades; *(below)* the funeral cortege, flanked by Cardiff firemen, leaving Pembroke Dock mortuary

186   Shand Ward, Cardiff Royal Infirmary, *c.*1905

187   Four officers of the Cardiff Battalion, Boys' Brigade, on the promenade at Porthcawl during camp, 1948. *(Left to right)* G. Powell, T. Cox, L. Cox, L. Griffiths

188 Guide G. Smith of the 1st Cardiff Company, taken by 'Dara, portrait specialist, St John Square', *c.*1910

189 Members of the 4th Cardiff Company, Girl Guides, at New Trinity Church, Theobald Road, Canton, in 1918

Memorable Events

190 A right royal welcome in Park Place for the 19 visit of King Edward VII and Queen Alexandra

191 Duke Street, a riot of colour with flags and bur ing, prepares for the royal visit in 1907

Roath.Park.Cardiff.1916

192   Wounded soldiers being entertained to a day-out at Roath Park with lady volunteers and boy scouts during the First World War

193   Limbless servicemen add a poignant touch to this show of patriotism in Sophia Gardens during the First World War

GOD BLESS OUR ALLIES

194 The south-west corner of the City Hall is just visible in this 1912 view of a distinguished gathering chatting animatedly during a break in proceedings of a now long-forgotten official occasion

195 A group of badger-baiting enthusiasts pose near the *Boar's Head*, Leckwith Road, *c*.1910. The man standing behind the case is John ('Jack') Morris

196 Captain Edward Tupper was an organiser for the National Sailors' and Firemen's Union and chief protagonist in the Cardiff Seamen's Strike of 1911 over low wages, Chinese and other foreign 'blackleg' labour. It was declared on 14 June and settled on 28 July

197 Newly-enlisted volunteers at Arms Park during the First World War. The Hippodrome in Westgate Street was showing 'The Wreck of the Birkenhead', a paddle steamer troopship lost in 1852 with great loss of life after striking an uncharted rock between Capetown and Port Elizabeth

198   Riverside Conservative Club outing in the 1920s

199   Employees of William Powell & Sons, provision merchants, Millicent Street, about to enjoy a staff outing, *c.*1930

200 Canton Conservative Club outing to Weston-super-Mare in 1959

201 Ely Brewery staff Christmas Party, 1950

202 Fancy Dress entrants at Mynachdy Flower Show, 1926

203 Eleven-year-old Mabel Hore was elected from all the Elementary schoolchildren of Cardiff to be the city's first Queen of the May in 1928. The revival of the ancient custom was organised by the Cardiff & District Branch of the Royal Society of St George in aid of the Royal Infirmary

204   Territorial Association (Welsh Field Ambulance) annual dance at the Carlton Rooms in 1938

205   The Welsh Miners' Choir, faces blackened with coal dust, sing their greetings to the Prince of Wales from the back of a Wadsworth's steam lorry outside the City Hall during the Royal Jubilee visit in 1935 *(see endpapers)*. The choir was leading a parade of floats depicting the 'Pageant of Industry'

206 Canton Conservative Club outing to Windsor in the late 1920s

207 King George VI and Queen Elizabeth inspecting members of No. 30 (F) Squadron, Air Defence Cadet Corps (forerunner of the Air Training Corps) in Cathays Park early in February 1940

208 Women's Junior Air Corps march past in Cathays Park, 1948

209 'VE Day' celebrations in Avon Street (formerly Halket Street), Canton, May 1945. Now demolished, the site is used as a car park

210 'VE Day' celebrations in Bradley Street, Roath, May 1945

211   'VE Day' celebrations in Cosmeston Street, Cathays, 1945

212   Rhiwbina's First Carnival Fete, 11 June 1949. The speaker is T. Pugsley, headmaster of
Rhiwbina School for many years

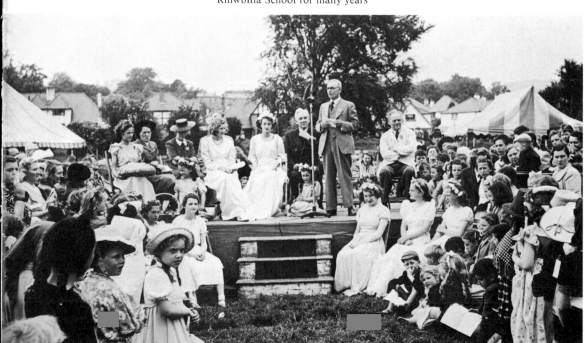

213/214   Residents of Llanmaes Street, Grangetown, celebrating the Coronation of
Queen Elizabeth II with a bumper street party in 1952